God's Amazing Everlasting Love

"A Biblical Study on the
Mercy, Forgiveness and Love of God."

"Forgive and you will be forgiven"
"Love Covers a Multitude of sins"
"Blessed are the Merciful"

John 3:16 "For God so loved the world, that He gave His only begotten Son, that whosoever believeth in Him, shall not perish, but shall have eternal life"

Heather Hope Johnson

authorHOUSE®

AuthorHouse™
1663 Liberty Drive
Bloomington, IN 47403
www.authorhouse.com
Phone: 1 (800) 839-8640

Published by AuthorHouse   01/23/2015

ISBN: 978-1-4969-6648-3 (sc)
ISBN: 978-1-4969-6647-6 (e)

"God loved us so much, He expressed His mercy and forgiveness by sending His son Jesus Christ, to die for our sins, so that we may live forever"

⁓   ⁓

All God asks of us is to

love Him in return

Contents

Acknowledgments

Certainly, the Lord is good and His mercies endure forever! It is with humility and great reverence that I honor and thank my Heavenly Father, my precious and loving Savior Jesus Christ and my Comforter, the Holy Spirit, for granting me the opportunity to scribe these divine words of hope and guidance. It was a lovely journey as the Scriptures unfolded and brought new light and new life. I know that I would not have been able to manifest this work without God's help and leadership. I am amazed by God's abundant love and awed by His powerful revelations. What an AWESOME GOD YOU ARE!

I am also extremely thankful to God for my awesome mother, D.M. Forbes Johnson, my phenomenal son K.A.M. Gray, and my first class brother H.C. Johnson. You have been such a profound blessing in my life, constantly encouraging me, teaching me and loving me through some tough seasons, yet never giving up on me. As I mature, I know for sure that family and the special people that God has blessed our lives with are more valuable compared to the accoutrements of life. Lessons taught by you will remain forever, yet to be passed on to others as my journey continues.

I shan't forget to thank all my spiritual family, my dear cousin Dr. O. Parris, all my awesome sisters in Christ, Pastors present and past, mother mentors, mentees, divine friendships designed by God, the WOFM Prayer Ministry Team, professors and all who have shared themselves with me over the years and even recently. Our relationship is more than what the natural eyes see and understand. Our meeting was divine and not in vain. I must remark that it is impossible for me to name each and every person in this book, however, you know the conversations we had, the prayers we prayed, the times shared momentarily or in transparency, the giggles and laughs, and even minor verbal spats, know for sure that you are an important part of my continuing journey with our awesome God. Thank you, thank you, and thank you!

Loving you……

Sister Heather Hope Johnson

Message to Readers

God bless you Family of God! Welcome to this Bible Study on God's Amazing Everlasting Love shown through mercy, forgiveness and love and how the three intersect each other. I believe that you are in for an exciting yet humbling and revelatory study as we journey and unravel the Scriptures together. We will learn that the love of God through Christ Jesus is foundational and the center piece of His mercy and forgiveness. When we discover God's amazing love in the very midst of our daily lives, we can chose to accept it, love the Lord in return and transcend love to others.

This study has been quite a personal one for me. In the past, I struggled with forgiving myself and others. I didn't understand mercy and underestimated God's forgiveness. I also wanted to learn the depth of God's love in new ways. Have you struggled with any of these three? Anybody? Somebody? Let's be honest shall we?

Family, this is an interactive study. There are many opportunities for you to do self-reflections, pen your own prayers and meditate on Scriptures. Make sure you take time to be still and listen to the voice of the Holy Spirit as He speaks specifically to you. Don't be afraid to cry or laugh. This too is a part of your process of healing and growing to the next level.

I pray that God will do a work in you as He has done with me. Our Lord knows how to transform our lives.

Let us pray:

"We now look to thee O Lord, to transform us from the inside out, as we learn about your great love for us, your mercy that endures forever and your forgiveness that frees us to lead a life that pleases you so that we can extend forgiveness, mercy and love to ourselves and others in Jesus name Amen."

Introduction

The church of the living and loving God is existing in a time where the people of God are exposed to a myriad of information whether it be good or evil. As believers, we are surrounded by perversions, idolatry, temptations, materialism, seduction and other anti-Christ situations. More than ever, the Disciples of Christ Jesus must be alert so as not to be swayed from the way and principles of Christ

In addition, believers ought not to be caught in negative events and negative cyclic pasts. We should learn to press forward and move past bad decisions that birthed negative outcomes. We should submit ourselves to prayer and be ever vigilant against spiritual plagues of ruminating negative thoughts, negative pasts and negative actions. One such plague is the spirit of un-forgiveness. Many cannot move forward because they are trapped by not choosing to forgive themselves and others of past wrongs. **<u>The truth is this: The master key that</u> <u>unlocks the dungeon of un-forgiveness is forgiveness.</u>** When we learn to forgive, we extend mercy. When we forgive and extend mercy, we walk in the spirit of love. There is no need to be paralyzed spiritually by something we do have control over. We all have the power to choose to forgive. We all have the power to choose to extend mercy. We all have the power to choose to love. The problem lies that we choose not to do the aforementioned to ourselves and to others. When we choose to forgive we free ourselves from the imprisonment of un-forgiveness.

Jesus showed us the way how to love. Jesus loved those who also rejected him. He came to His own but His own received Him not, but that did not stop His mission and His purpose to love. He laid down His life so that whosoever believeth in Him would not perish but have everlasting life.

Our Savior taught us how to show mercy and forgiveness by the parables He taught in the Gospels. Jesus knew that we would have to learn how to forgive not once, but continuously. He is the greatest example of mercy, forgiveness and love. He forgave a harlot, a betrayer and us.

Forgiving, showing mercy and loving is not impossible to do. It takes the power and spirit of God to show us how. I urge you to surrender to Jesus Christ our Savior today. Whether you are a believer or not, we all struggle with issues of loving, showing mercy and rendering forgiveness.

Journey through this study and access the Lord's power at work in you to forgive, show mercy and love.

The Sin Issue

We live in a world where sin is at times practiced daily in the lives of unbelievers and believers alike. The truth is this according to the word of God:

"All have sinned and have fallen short of the glory of God."

None of us are totally living free from sin. We have to ask God to forgive us from sins each day. What really is sin? Sin is any act that God declares wrong. So if any man thinks that a particular action is right in his eyes, but God declares it as wrong as revealed in the Holy Scriptures, then it is wrong. It doesn't matter what man believes, thinks or perceives as correct when it comes to sin. **What God says is sin is simply what it is: SIN.** The Scriptures also states that if we know to do right, and not do it, it is also considered as sin. Any sin we have committed in error or intentionally must be brought to God, by confession and asking Him to forgive us.

Sin occurred in the Garden of Eden when Adam **<u>disobeyed</u>** the command of God. Adam was told not to eat of the fruit from the tree of knowledge of good and evil. This seemed like a simple enough command, yet, this command carried a consequence if disobeyed. **<u>Consequence: They would die</u>**. There is one thing that all should know about the sin issue: It brings death. Death has many forms, physical and spiritual. Death, simply put, is the cessation of life. In Adam's and Eve's case, sin brought a separation, a death, an interruption in the flow and the intimate life relationship with God.

It is natural of mankind to have the propensity to do the wrong thing, to disobey and to sin. God also knows that He has also wired us to choose to obey, but it is simply our choice. **Choice is ours to manage. Consequence is God's power to issue**. Whenever we sin, which is choosing to do wrong versus the right, remember that there are consequences waiting for us to deal with. God will not force us to obey Him or His directives, for God wants us to choose to love Him. Forced love is not true love. If we love God, then we will obey His commandments. If we choose to love and obey something else or someone else other than God, then we have chosen to obey the leading of that person or that thing. Not loving God is choosing to love something or someone else other than God. I link this with the command God gave: **"Love the Lord your God with all your heart, mind, soul and strength."**

I believe that if we truly practice this daily, to love God with our all, then loving sin or anything else will not have a strong hold on us.

I have learned that because God loves us dearly, He knows what is best for us and He desires that we come into agreement with His plans and desires for our lives. He is our Creator and therefore the Creator knows what is best for what He has created. Why would God create with the intent to destroy? God knows what each of us are made of physically, emotionally, and spiritually. He knows what we can and cannot handle. **God knows that He didn't design us to handle sin. Sin steals, kills and destroy.** God doesn't want us to destroy ourselves ever so slowly and terminally because of the effects of sin. Jesus came so that we may have life and have life more abundantly. That's why God gave us life, to live, to enjoy, to love, and to last. Despite the systems in place in this world to wreak havoc in our lives, it is still possible to live life more abundantly right here and right now. It is a matter of choice to invite sin in or reject it out of our lives.

<u>**Self Reflection**</u>: *Face sin, in order to have God help us fix sin!*

Think about the ways you have sinned in the past and how you are sinning presently. Document sin in your life by listing a few of them in your personal journal or below:

1._____ 2._____ 3._____ 4._____ 5._____

Look at these and ask yourself: How can these sins affect my life now or in the future? Can any of these sin wreck my life or the lives of others such as children or a spouse? What are the possible consequences of these sins? Journalize your answers privately.

—•—

The thing about sin is this**: It hurts us and oftentimes others**. ***The major purpose of sin is to separates us from God.*** Now this separation is not God's fault, taking a leave of absence and leaving us to waddle in our mud of sin. God will not leave us or forsake us, but the sin which we partake of is what drives an invisible wedge between us and God. In other words, we are the ones who decide to rest under the influence of sin by choosing to introduce an ungodly act that breaks in and stands in between us and God. The sin we partake of takes a preferential position in our lives. **Rather than us preferring God we prefer sin**.

EXAMPLE: US ←------------ SIN------------→ GOD

The other thing about sin is this: It masks itself as enjoyable, fascinating, feeding the flesh negatively, yet starving and hurting mankind spiritually, emotionally, and physically. One of my mentors told me years ago*: Satan makes sin seem sweet*. In other words: **Sin seems delicious. Sin seduces. It seems to satisfy……..yet sin**

stings. This is true. Sin can bite you so hard it can leave a lasting reminder and mark in your life.

—•—

We see the outcome of sin in the lives of many on a daily basis. Look around and tune into how sin messes up many in this world. Drug addicts are chasing the high of drugs such as cocaine and ecstasy, yet eventually, we observe how the same drug that brings temporary elation, tears away at a drug user's body, mind and spirit. The sin of drug abuse brings some users to homelessness, prostitution and even death. The point is this: **Sin hurts mankind**. It appeals falsely to the human needs. **Sin seduces and gives a false impression to satisfy the human cravings**. It only masks itself as fulfilling, only to damage, torment and end the lives of human beings.

Journeys of Sin in the Scriptures

From Genesis and throughout the trajectory of the lives of many in the Scriptures, we see sin disabling and mangling the lives of many. Let's mention a few here:

1. Cain **killed** Able.

2. Moses **killed** an Egyptian.

3. David's **adultery** with Bathsheba and the **murder** of Uriah

4. Potiphar's wife **lies** on Joseph because she wanted to commit adultery

5. The **rape** of Tamar by her brother

6. Judas **betrayal** of Jesus

7. Peter's **denial** of knowing Jesus **(lying)**

What are some of the sins you are aware of scripturally that aren't mentioned above?

If you notice the list above, sin affects the sinner as well as the person sinned against. **Sin also casts invisible chains of bondage on the lives of people**. These chains are unseen to the naked eye, but we can see the effects of bondage on the lives of people. Yet, God offers hope for mankind. God does not want sinners to be lost, hopeless or bound by sin. He wants sinners saved. **God's solution for a world of sinners and sin is: JESUS.** God, wrapped in the flesh, came to this world as-EMMANUEL-God with us, to die for us, to regain and remain with us.

Satan-the Craftsman of Sin

Satan's, the chief enemy of God is the craftsman of sin. Sin was not designed by God. Our enemy and God's enemy, Satan, wants mankind to conceive sin, birth it, nurse it and have it feed on us for as long as we choose sin versus choosing God. The major thing Satan doesn't want us to do, is to bring sin to the light-God's Light. Sin is oftentimes performed in secrecy and darkness, away from the light- away from God's revealing light. We need to shine the light on sin.

Why should we shine the Light on sin?

Friends, learn this truth: **The stronghold of sin is secrecy and darkness**. Satan wants us to suffer silently under the stronghold of sin that sucks the life out of us. It is time, even now, to command sin out of the dark areas of our lives and have God shine His glorious light on it. In doing so, we gain freedom from sin and its sick secretive ways. Whenever we sin, we must do as First John 1 vs. 7 to 10:

*"But if we walk in the light as He is in the light, we have fellowship with one another, and the blood of Jesus Christ His Son **cleanses** us from all sin. If we say that we have no sin, we deceive ourselves, and the truth is not in us. **If we confess our sins, He is faithful and just to forgive us our sins and to cleanse us from all unrighteousness.** If we say that we have not sinned, we make Him a liar, and His word is not in us."*

Heather Hope Johnson

We notice the word **"cleanse"** in this Scripture passage. It is clear that sin makes us unclean. In other words: **Sin messes us up, and therefore we need to get clean with God for our own good.** In order to be cleansed from sin, we must confess we have sinned. The above Scripture is also clear that we cannot lie and state that we do not sin. It has also heralded that we cannot say that we sin and also walk in the light and fellowship with God, for we understand that sin breaks that fellowship and brings us into darkness. It is best for us to not deceive ourselves. How can we say we are not sinning when we know that we are? It is best to be truthful, face the music, face our pure and perfect loving God honestly and confess our sins. When we ask God to forgive us, he will cleanse us from all the filth that sin marks us with.

Many people refuse to confess that they have done something wrong. If we refuse to face the truth of the error of our ways, how can we gain freedom? Don't believe that your way is the truth to receive God's freedom from sin. We need to live and do things Gods way to gain Godly freedom. Believe God's truth and God's way. Your viewpoint of righteousness often will not align to God's standard of righteousness. If you chose to be god of your life that is your choice. If you choose God's truth, then confess your sins to God and see how freedom will come into your life and you will be transformed.

Friends, my advice to you is this: **Don't play around with sin in your life**. I am teaching from experience. It is burdensome, dirty, blinding and suffocating. I have experienced the torment of sinning and having to deal with the torment and guilt.

Many believers have experienced the weight of sin. I very much disliked the burden, trouble, grief and unsettling in my spirit, all because of sin. Sin plagues and attacks the mind and has the ability to morph you from the inside out. I had to face the sins and then confess them to God. The enemy of sin I was fighting was real, however, not a tangible one. The Lord strategically led me to specific people whom I had to reach out to for help. They were not surprised, neither were they judgmental, for they too understood my burden. Why? They too had endured a season of the same sin and now were equipped to be transparent with me and to help me overcome. I tell you this because: Sin is sin in God's eyes even when we try to rationalize it. You see, the evil we fight wants us to rationalize sins. Then it will try to make you think that the sin is not *"that bad compared to what other people are doing"*. Don't believe it! God knows what our weaknesses are, yet He doesn't want us to hide and suffer secretly and rationalize it. We need to be led by God to the person or people who He trusts and who we can confide in to help us pray for strength to get free from the chains of sin. When we team up with God and with others who have overcome specific sinful ways, we gain strength to overcome. Freedom for us also means freedom for others. God will use us and our experiences to minister to those who struggle with the same sin issue. Know this for sure family: **<u>Every issue of sin, once freed, can be used for ministry.</u>** One of my dear sisters in Christ taught me this: **God can take a mistake and can turn it into a sweepstake**! Even now, think about the sins that have been trying to keep you captive. Let us pray about them now.

Prayer: Be Set Free from all types of sin and condemnation in Jesus name.

"Heavenly Father, I thank you that you don't hold sins against us forever. You came to set the captives free from all types of sinful actions. Because you want me to live a life free from condemnation and sin, you said that I must confess my sins to you. Lord, I confess to you the sins of:_____ _____ and I am asking you Lord to shut down and shut out all these sinful actions out of my mind, body, spirit and being so I can live in total freedom from them from this day forward. Lord I am depending on you to help me to move forward from darkness into your light in Jesus name amen"

Now take some time and meditate on what you have read and pray to God and ask God to give you the strength to turn away completely from those sins and to never invite them into your life again.

Attributes of Forgiveness, Mercy and Love

Earlier we learned that many people struggle with rendering forgiveness to others. I personally know people who have had issues on the job, hating and blaming a supervisor for wrongs committed against them. I know families torn apart because of money issues that drove a wedge of un-forgiveness between siblings. I have seen children who cast parents aside because of something that happened years ago. I too had issues with un-forgiveness within my family, but thankfully, those issues were settled and we overcame those bitter hurdles. In order to understand forgiveness, we need to look closely at un-forgiveness.

Self-Reflect: How would you define un-forgiveness?

In your own words define un-forgiveness:

_____

_____

Do you identify any un-forgiveness in your heart against another? Journalize them:_____**How has un-forgiveness affected your life? Your health? Does it bother you often, occasionally or seasonally?**

_____

In reflecting, I am sure you can trace un-forgiveness to an offense. This offense may or may not be sinful, but it is often attached to someone offending another. Let's face it, there are millions even billions of people who struggle with un-forgiveness. Are you one? Honestly, are you a person who holds on to grudges, offenses, malice and hatred? We need to look within in order to face any type of dysfunction. When we can be honest with ourselves, then we can move forward to be released from bondage.

The reasons for the occurrences of un-forgiveness are vast. Reasons range from a lie, adultery, stolen property, a nasty comment, murder, rape, gossip, cheating, scheming or any other situation that can cut the very spiritual heart core of others. When people are deeply hurt they can hold on to offenses for years. Some people die with them. My question is this: ***Is it really worth it?***

Your response might be: "Sister, you have no idea what "so and so did to me".

My response to that is: "So and so may just be living their life, having a jolly good time, while you are stewing in the pressure cooker of un-forgiveness"

The Holy Spirit revealed to me something simple about un-forgiveness. When we hold on to hurts by shutting people out of our lives either by malice or other ways, just to prove to them that "you don't deserve my friendship and I will make you pay by not having anything to do with you" then all we are doing is drinking poison and expecting the offender to die. Never in a million years will we prove a point by hating. Hate, grudges, malice and such do not solve issues. We will learn later that it is love that solves problems. Jesus taught us that "Love conquers all" even if it means loving people at length.

Earlier, you were assigned to define un-forgiveness. My personal definition of un-forgiveness is this:

"Holding an offence committed against us in our heart, mind, body and spirit for an undetermined amount of time in order to prove that the offender has committed a grave offense and is not deserving of pardon"

In other words, the offender must be punished (often severely) by the offended for the offense committed.

Most human beings have a nature within them to react negatively rather than respond positively to offenses. Whether we react privately or publicly is another issue. We see this reaction to offenses even in the lives of children as young as four years old, who seek to use revenge on other children who have offended them. Where do children learn revenge from? Have they been taught by their parent's example or could it be an innate trait tracing their behaviors to the sin nature?

We have learned that un-forgiveness has a strong link with revenge, malice, anger and stored hatred. **Now what do you think God thinks about un-forgiveness? Do you think we have a right to NOT forgive others? Do you think we should issue revenge in any form we please to teach offenders lessons? Do you think stored hatred in our heart is healthy? Journalize your responses.**

_____

_____

Personal Reflection

I remember a time in my life I had stored hatred in my heart for two specific individuals who were unrelated to each other but we shared a unique relationship. The relationship with each party turned sour and in my estimation, they hurt me deeply. I valued and loved them much and so I didn't think that what transpired between us would have ever happened. I couldn't understand how people could treat others with such cutting actions and words. I wanted nothing to do with them when the relationship frayed for I decided to go about my merry way and leave them to their own path. Yet, I was secretly angry on the inside and I just couldn't shake it. Then God stepped in and had a one to one conversation with me in regards to the un-forgiveness that was stored in my heart which was bothering me to bits and pieces. You see, we can never hide from God and His Sovereignty. God knows all that we are dealing with and because God knows what is good for us, he steps in to heal us from bitterness to betterment. I have learned that the Lord will deal with us gently to face hidden problems so that we can overcome them and rise to new levels. God showed me that I still harbored negative feelings toward these individuals and I hadn't forgiven them. Yes, they had hurt me, but I also had my share of inflicting hurt on them. Yes, the relationships frayed, because God was rearranging and doing new things in my life, so I had to understand that no matter what I faced, who treated me how, God is still in control and is Master and Mediator of my life. He knew I needed to learn valuable lessons of forgiveness in order to move forward. The Lord instructed me to ***"Forgive them from my heart, to truly forgive them."*** Read that statement again***. "Forgive them from your heart. Truly forgive them."*** Do you know how many people are walking around daily, stating they have forgiven others, but really haven't truly forgiven them? Are you one of them? Reflect now and listen to the Holy Spirit. Is there anyone the Lord is bringing to your spirit or your mind now? If yes, then you need to ***"truly forgive that person from your heart"***. Pause, breathe and say a prayer from your heart now. Ask the Lord God, in the name of Jesus, to help you to truly release and forgive that person for offending you. Name the offense specifically and ask the Lord to heal you right now from the pain, the anguish, the torment and the tears you have endured because of that offense. If you need to, journalize or write a letter to God.

~•~

Wounds from offences that causes un-forgiveness run deep. They are like entangled roots of a tree deep under the earth. In order to demolish the root of un-forgiveness, we need to untangle it and truly forgive. God has shown me that when we live in a mode of un-forgiveness, we will lose our peace, joy, and it can also affect our health and finances. A hardened heart of un-forgiveness turns in different directions to find happiness and peace. I remember there was a time I couldn't breathe or sleep well due to my choice in carrying an unnecessary baggage of un-forgiveness in my heart. Un-forgiveness is a spirit that keeps us hostage from the freedom God wants us to live in. Un-forgiveness is burdensome and the only answer to this locked suitcase of "heavy issues" is the key of forgiveness that opens it. We must choose to empty out its contents and throw them all away!

<u>Choosing to Forgive</u>

Forgiveness is the key that opens spiritual doors and releases us from the bondage of un-forgiveness, however, we must **CHOOSE TO FORGIVE**! Forgiveness not only opens doors, but it also moves us strategically into positions to extend mercy and love to others. Yes, the person who did you that wrong was evil, bitter, vicious, heartless, criminal and tyrannical but the point is this: *Are you hurting them any more than you are hurting yourself by hating them for the rest of your life?* Go ahead, answer the question. You, my dear, listen well: *Hating that person who did you wrong will not change anything that happened in the past.* **Is hating them now making the situation better? No. But hating them may be clogging your life, your health, your flow of blessing to come to you.** Listen, I am not suggesting that you have to be best friends with someone who hurt you. Oftentimes it is best to be far away from that person for your own good, but hating them and never ever forgiving them for the rest of your life is not hurting them. You are only hurting yourself.

It is not the easiest thing to forgive, but we must trust God's word that forgiving is a safe haven for us. **Read what Jesus said in Matthew 6 vs 14 -15:**

"For <u>if you forgive men their trespasses, your heavenly Father will also forgive you. But if you do not forgive men their trespasses, neither will your Father forgive your trespasses</u>"

What do you understand about what Jesus said about forgiveness in this passage? Journalize your thoughts here or in your private journal.

_____

I believe that this verse is as strict and as heavy as the commandment to love God and to love others. The direction is quite clear in this verse, but quite difficult to do by believers and unbelievers alike. I believe that satan has trapped many people in the spirit of un-forgiveness. You see, satan's objective is to use deception to have us fall into the ditch of un-forgiveness. ***<u>When we become stubborn and sit on the throne of un-forgiveness, we unknowingly lock ourselves out of the blessings of the Father's forgiveness.</u>*** You see, much blessings come with forgiveness. We hold on to our blessings of peace, joy, health, our right mind, freedom to live and enjoy life and so much more when we choose to forgive. On the other hand, un-forgiveness robs us of all those blessings and more. Is that what you want to happen to you? Look at the verse again. Let's pull the first statement apart and analyze it.

Vs;14 "If you forgive men their trespasses..." This is a conditional statement because it begins with the word "if". This means ***"if you choose to do a thing then***

there will be a result based off of your choice". Hence, ***if you or I choose to forgive men when they offend us THEN "our heavenly Father will also forgive us"***

In other words: When we choose to forgive those who offend us, then God will forgive us of our offences as well, especially, offences against Him.

Vs:15 "But if you do not forgive men their trespasses, neither will your Father forgive your trespasses." This too is a conditional statement, because it has the word "if". We see that there is the word "but" before the word "if", which contrast the first conditional statement. Here we see ***that those who choose NOT to forgive men their offenses, they will NOT receive forgiveness from our Heavenly Father for their trespasses.*** This part of the statement rests mostly in the hands of those who choose not to do what is required. Much like Cain bringing an offering to God that God wasn't pleased with, therefore it was rejected. Ever since the beginning, the Genesis of the world, God desires that we remain in the right state of heart. God always sees what's going on in our hearts. God says to forgive from our hearts. If we choose not to forgive, then God will reject requests for forgiveness when we ask it of Him. ***This will totally be the fault and burden for those who choose to NOT pardon others, for they will NOT receive pardon.*** God cannot be blamed when people live in un-forgiveness. They are the ones hurting themselves unnecessarily because they choose not to forgive. **Forgiveness gives us freedom**. *Un-forgiveness guarantees us bondage.* God has scribed in the Scriptures as a reminder to us that in order to receive forgiveness from God, we will have to forgive those who have offended us.

Teammates: Mercy and Forgiveness

You rarely see the spirit of forgiveness at work without seeing its very good friend which is **mercy**. Jesus taught a parable about an unforgiving servant. Let us take a look at this parable in **Matthew 18 vs. 23 to 35** where you will witness the head of mercy resting at the heartbeat of forgiveness. We will see also how it ties in with the **Scripture Matthew 6 vs. 14-15.**

Attributes of Mercy-The Unforgiving Servant

Read Matthew 18 vs. 23 -35

What were some of the key phrases, words or sections that ministered directly to you? Journalize them.

In this parable, we see where a king was settling debts owed to him by servants. A particular servant owed the king a large amount, however, the servant was not in a position to satisfy this debt. The king executed a judgment to have the servant sold along with his wife, children and all that he had. This was quite a desperate and discouraging position for this servant and I can even imagine how anxious and fearful this servant became. This servant begged the king to have patience with him and gave the king his promise that he would pay all that he owed. The servant took a humbling position by falling at the feet of the king begging desperately. Can you imagine how he probably cried miserably, possibly holding out his hands towards the king begging him to accept his request to be patient with him? Now something happened in verse 27.

The Scripture reads:

"**Then the master (king) of that servant was _moved with compassion, released him_, and _forgave him_ the debt.**"

This verse is an exceptional verse and there is so much we can learn from it. Before we do so, answer these questions: **Why do you think the king changed his mind? What moved the king?**

_____

We may never know what exactly moved the heart of the king to make this change, but we know that the hearts of kings are in the Hand of the Lord to move it to and fro to make decision wherever He pleases. We can surmise that it is after what the servant did in verse 26 that had a direct impact on the change of the king's decisions. **The verse states**:

"The servant therefore fell down before the him, saying, 'Master, have patience with me, and I will pay you all'"

This position of **falling to the feet** of the king was a position of "worship". It is amazing how worship can change a situation. Who knows? Maybe the king saw the sincerity or desperation in the servant as he begged and pleaded for patience. Possibly, the king knew that it was impossible for the servant to pay such a large owing and so relieved him of that exorbitant debt. Could it be when the king looked upon the servant, had a moment or a flashback and was reminded that he too needed compassion and forgiveness for unpaid debts others knew nothing about? What the king offered to the servant is worthy to remember. The king extended **compassion (mercy)** and **forgiveness** to a servant who owed a huge debt. If the king hadn't extended this to the servant then that servant would have had to take a lifetime to pay the debt. Thankfully, the king resolved to forgive him of it and cast it away from the servant.

We see also in this parable our very own lives. Here we are living a life loaned to us by God and as we live it, we rack up a tab of debt. Sin debt. The thing about sin as we have learned is this: Sin has consequences. Sin brings death and destruction and somebody has to pay the bill. There comes a time in our lives that every deed we have done we will have to answer for someday. This is what God calls Judgment Day. We will all be judged on this day. The servant's "judgment day" came to pay his debt. This is what the Scriptures call "brought to account" in verse 24 and for the servant, his debt was a HUGE one. How big is your bill….your sin debt that is? Can you pay it off before Judgment day? Probably not and you don't need to, for a King has paid it already for you. King Jesus! The servant couldn't pay his bill and neither can we. This is why the king decided to have compassion on the servant and forgave him of every penny he owed. This is why God had compassion on us also, forgave us of our sins and paid our sin debt for us through the crucifixion, death, burial and resurrection of Jesus Christ. Jesus, the Son of God, laid His life down, to grant us a new life in Him. Jesus paid the sin debt for us, for He knew that it would be impossible for us to pay it on our own. If you think you can pay the sin debt yourself, think again. Jesus already gave you the choice to accept His sacrifice of love as your sin debt **<u>PAID IN FULL</u>**. Will you accept His mercy and forgiveness for your sins? Are you saved? Do you believe what Jesus did for you is worth accepting?

If you aren't a spirit filled believer in Christ Jesus, the Son of the Living God, and you want to accept the finished work and gift of salvation that Christ paid for you pray this prayer with me now:

"Heavenly Father, I know that you love me and you paid an enormous sin debt so that I can have eternal life in Christ Jesus. Forgive me of all my sins. Come into my heart. Be the center of my life. Make me new and help me to live the life you designed just for me. Thank you for your sacrifice, mercy, forgiveness and love. This I pray in Jesus name amen."

May the Spirit of the Lord fill your life and lead you into His paths of righteousness peace and love, protecting you daily, showering you with His favor, love and blessings and speaking to you specifically about the plans He has designed just for you. This I declare for you in Jesus name Amen.

***You are now a new person in Christ Jesus. Ask the Lord to lead you to the correct church, so that the new Spirit of God that lives in you will be built and edified.

Let us continue our journey with the Unmerciful Servant.

We see that the servant was forgiven of a huge debt, but his heart wasn't changed. He received an awesome gift of forgiveness, but his heart wasn't impacted by the gift of forgiveness to extend what he received to another. This servant refused to forgive another. **Read Matthew 18 vs. 28-30**

<u>**The Unmerciful Servant Refuses to Forgive**</u>

Matthew 18 verses 28 to 30.

After reading verses 28 to 30, what spoke to your heart about this servant? Journalize here._____

_____

In these few verses we see the dynamics of this parable take a swift shift. The same servant who was *"released"* from an enormous debt by the king who showed compassion towards him, came across one of his fellow servants who owed him one hundred pence. The unmerciful servant grabbed hold of his fellow servant and demanded payment of debt owed immediately. The fellow servant however had to beg by pleading for patience to pay his debt. Note here, that the fellow servant also went at the feet of the servant begging, however, no mercy was given by the unmerciful servant and the fellow servant was thrown into prison until the debt was paid. Let us pause here and analyze.

Would you say that this was an identical situation between the king and unmerciful servant and the two servants? How do the two scenarios differ? What can you personally learn from these two scenarios? Journalize.

_____

It is discouraging that as human beings, it is often so easy for us to forget kindness extended to us by others. Here we see the unmerciful servant standing in a position of creditor to his fellow servant. It wasn't too long before he was at the feet of the king as a debtor. We see where the unmerciful servant found it hard to relieve his fellow servant of a debt that was a feebly portion to what he owed previously to the king. Although the fellow servant was at the feet of the unmerciful servant begging, that didn't move his heart to show compassion, but rather his heart chose to throw his fellow servant in prison. We may all turn up our noses at this unmerciful servant and be quick to judge him, but you will be surprised how you and I are guilty of the same actions this unmerciful servant committed. We all tend to do the same things at times, whether it be subtly or harshly. Before we continue allow me to share with you a time when I too was unforgiving to others.

A Personal Reflection of Un-forgiveness

Being un-forgiving to others, as was done by that unmerciful servant, is not news to any of us. We are guilty of it as well. On reading the Scripture, I remember a time when I was enduring some really hard trials and my life was a struggle even as a believer loving the Lord. I had a major shift in my life where God released me from a bitter abusive second marriage and I had relocated to an apartment God blessed me with. I was also adjusting on my own with my son who was a teen at that time. This adjustment was a deep long process for us both. Internally, I was hurt and broken, yet, if others on the outside viewed my life it would look "all together". It was not. I needed healing in every possible area in my life from my heart to my finances and what I was bearing was slowly affecting my health through colds, a nagging cough and restless nights. Silently, I was angry at life. I still praised God, prayed and read my Word for I was determined to start over from the bottom and rise again to the zenith. In enduring the healing process, I wanted my life to evolve quickly, but God was showing me that I had un-forgiveness in my heart for the two men I had formally married. I couldn't understand how I showed love to these two men at different junctures of my life, but in my perspective they didn't value the love I gave. Then God blew out the candles of my **"I am not at fault cake"** God showed me that yes, I was loving to these men, but I hadn't listened and obeyed God's directives, prior to and during both marriages. My first marriage ended due to stubbornness on my part for I was **un-willing to forgive this man for erring and thinking that our first child was illegitimate.** We had gotten married very young and gotten pregnant not long after. During my pregnancy, we lived apart because he was an active serviceman in another state. He was soon to leave the service to be home with the family, however, when our son was born, he thought that our son didn't belong to him due to the child's skin color. That was extremely hurtful on my end and therefore I took off on my own, trying to prove a point that I didn't need him as a husband. Although he tried to make amends, I chose to hold on to anger and revenge. I refused to forgive him for even thinking that I would cheat on him and bring a child into a marriage that wasn't his. Un-forgiveness broke the marriage apart and we went our ways into other hurtful relationships that also ended due to un-forgiveness. Years went by with un-forgiveness nested in my heart and I entered into a second marriage with unresolved issues. The second marriage I entered was definitely not designed by God but was designed by two broken people looking for comfort and support on different levels. The relationship was more like a mortal combat where we fought practically every day over anything despite how insignificant it was. God had used many people to warn me about the fatal position I was in, but I was determined to prove people wrong. I tried to convince myself the marriage would work but I knew deep inside that it wouldn't and ignored all the warning signs. I almost lost my life. God had to step in, practically backed me against a wall, showed me one door for escape and that was the way God delivered me out of that dangerous dysfunctional relationship. Another shadow of un-forgiveness nested in my heart, but God was at work as he placed me in a season of restoration and healing. During this season, God showed me that because I didn't forgive my first husband, I created an atmosphere of un-forgiveness that walk right into a second marriage that wasn't God's will, but man's doing. When the second marriage ended God showed me that I had to let go and forgive both men. I had to be willing to forgive and free them of all the negative offenses, words, actions, revenge and spite so that I would be free to engage in a correct heart-set and mindset for any existing and future relationships God had in store for me. I also had to learn how to forgive myself for not obeying the instructions of God as it relates to making decisions. It took a while for me to forgive myself. I blamed myself for many happenings and was disappointed at the trajectory of my life. Then I heard a quote that turned my life upward: ***"Guilt is the biggest waste of time."*** This guilt however was guilt of the past where I wished I had listened and done what I was being guided to do. I knew I couldn't change the past, but I grew stronger from it. The many experiences I had I now use to help many women to see God in their circumstances and observe how God is able to restore and renew lives. The biggest lesson I learned was to forgive and move forward because God still can accomplish His purpose in my life, but I needed to let go of the past and the pain.

You see God wants us to be free in extending mercy and forgiveness to others. What breeds in our hearts is the atmosphere we create for now and the future. If our heart is contaminated, we contaminate relationships that exist or will exist. If our heart is free and forgiving, we enter into relationships accordingly. I am proud to say that although it took time to shed the layers of pain and hurt due to un-forgiveness, I know that it was well worth it to release all offences committed against me because I know that I am not perfect and I too did hurtful things to these men through words and actions.

Reflection: Is your heart breeding un-forgiveness? Ask the Holy Spirit to search your heart to locate any un-forgiveness or un-mercifulness breeding there. Pray and ask God to release you of it now. Journalize and write your pr ayer._____

Let us continue with the unmerciful servant and how his heart revealed itself to others. His actions were noticed how he treated his fellow servant and a judgment was pronounced because of his unforgiving behavior.

The Unmerciful Servant is Noticed and Judged.

Read Matthew 18 vs. 31 to 35

The actions of the unmerciful servant was noticed and dealt with. It is amazing that when we act in ways that are unloving and unkind, thinking that no one sees us, know for sure that God is watching. God notices all that we do and He has a way of showing us up. That is exactly what happened to this unmerciful servant. His actions towards his fellow servant was noticed and was reported.

Verse 31-34 states:

"So when his fellow servants saw what had been done, they were grieved and came and told their master all that had done. Then his master, after he had called him, said to him, "You wicked servant! I forgave you all that debt because you begged me. Should you not also have had compassion on your fellow servant, just as I had pity on you?'

We see here that those who saw how the servant treated his fellow servant were grieved in their hearts. **Know this for sure: Whatever grieves the heart of man, <u>God is even <u>more grieved and displeased about it.</u></u>** Just as how the king called the servant "wicked" God identifies and is displeased by wicked actions. The king was told that the unmerciful-servant did not treat his fellow servant kindly. In essence this unmerciful servant didn't treat the one owing him money in a way he would have wanted to be treated. ***There is a Golden Rule that has been given to us. We must treat people the way we would like to be treated. This translates love.*** The unmerciful servant lacked this element of love in his heart and opted to punish his fellow servant for a debt that he could have forgiven. God will always step into situations and bring corrections to unjust, unloving, unkind and wicked actions.

Verse 34-35 states:

"And his master was angry, and delivered him to the torturers until he should pay all that was due to him. *So My heavenly Father also will do to you if each of you, from his heart, does not forgive his brother his trespasses*"

A holy anger came upon the king to the extent that he did a number of things that turned the life of the unmerciful servant from release and freedom into torment and bondage. **The king:**

1.   **Reinstated the debt.**

2.   **Delivered the unmerciful servant to the torturers**.

Can you imagine what was going through this unmerciful servant's mind? Here he was back in a position he was delivered from, but now he would be tortured. All of this occurred because he refused to forgive, refused to extend mercy and refused to love. This too will happen to us if we choose the route of non-compassion, non-mercy and not extending love to those whom we ought to forgive.

I believe the unmerciful servant positioned himself in jeopardy all because he forgot too fast. He was released from a large debt, but this act of love on the king's part towards him didn't move his heart enough for him to extend likewise love, mercy and forgiveness to another who was indebted to him. Let it not be us. When we think we can get away with the evil we do to others, we won't, because the report will end up in the hearing of our God, our Judge, our Master and our King.

In verse 35, Jesus states what will happen to those who choose not to forgive. Complete the Scripture below by filling in the blanks.

"So, My heavenly _____ also will _____ _____ _____ if each of _____ from _____ _____ does not _____ his brother his _____."

This Scripture above embraces Matthew 6 vs 14-15. Read it and fill in the blanks.

"For if you _____ men their trespasses, your heavenly Father _____you. But if you do not _____ men their trespasses, neither will your _____

trespasses."

Forgiveness is a **CHOICE**. It is an act of **MERCY and LOVE from the HEART**. If we choose to truly forgive **we will not be held CAPTIVE** neither will we be **TORMENTED for not FORGIVING. (Read this phrase about 3 times)**

Let us pray: "Heavenly Father, help me Lord to be a merciful and forgiving person. Help me to choose to forgive from my heart, to extend mercy, to have patience with others, for in doing so I will extend love and live free from torment. Search my heart today and do a work in me Lord. Thank you for showing me in your word that blessed are the merciful, because they will be shown mercy. This I pray in Jesus name. Amen."

Jesus, His Love, Mercy and Forgiveness

Throughout the Scriptures, we see the amazing love, forgiveness and the mercy of God in action constantly towards mankind. Jesus showed loved to many. Whether the person was a child, a prostitute, a thieving tax collector, the demon possessed, the blind, the lame or the dumb, Jesus loved them. God still continues to love those who are tormented and suffering whether it be silently or openly. **<u>The point is this: We are living in an imperfect world with people who are hurt and broken, but GOD LOVES THEM.</u>** Millions of people from different types of cultures are facing all sorts of issues that have brought sorrow and chaos into their lives. We can pause and reflect on our past and some of the issues we had to face and somehow connect with some of the issues people face today. The sad thing is: Many choose to forget what they have been delivered from and are so busy with their lives they don't try to reach out and help another. Extending a helping hand of mercy and love doesn't always mean to give money. We can take time to pray for or with others in need, spend a few minutes with someone struggling with hopelessness, give some sort of encouragement or invite someone to church or to your home for dinner. **Love is shown in what we do and not only what we say**. **Love is being proactive and responding to needs.** This is what Jesus did and as Believers we are to do the same. Let us take a look at a Scripture that showed how Jesus was proactive and responsive to the need of a woman caught in the act of adultery.

An Adulteress Faces the Light of the World

Read John 8 vs 1 -12. Meditate on the Scripture.

What were some of the key words, phrases or emotions that you noticed in this Scripture? Journalize your entry.

_____

In this biblical event we see an adulterous woman who came face to face with Jesus, the Light of the world. She was about her private personal sexual affairs and was caught in the act and brought to Jesus. Isn't it amazing how at times when we are about our business, we end up getting caught? Why? God has a way of interrupting our course of life to appoint us a different course for our good and His glory. This is what happened to her.

Not only was she caught and brought to Jesus, she was in the midst of the temple where other people were. Can you imagine how she felt? The shame, the regret, the horror of those eyes looking at her with disdain and hatred. She must have been nervous for she knew the consequences…..being stoned to death.

There was another dynamic at work. The Pharisees and Scribes who dragged this woman into the temple to face Jesus was up to something. They had planned not only to bring accusation to this woman and her sinful behaviors, but they also wanted to accuse Jesus. Accusations were the theme of this event by these scribes and Pharisees, not knowing that Jesus already knew their intentions. John 8 vs 4 to 6 states what the Pharisees and scribes said to Jesus in the presence of others:

"Teacher, this woman was caught in adultery, in the very act. Now Moses, in the law, commanded us that such should be stoned. But what do you say?" ***This they said, testing Him, that they might have something of which to accuse Him.*** **But Jesus stooped down and wrote on the ground with His finger <u>as though He did not hear.</u>"**

It is amazing how people are often ready to point fingers at others for wrong doings, but forget to remember their own hidden faults. Although according to the Law of Moses this woman was condemned to death because of her sinful action, the Pharisee didn't realized that Jesus knew all about the law. He was the Law Giver and the true Judge of the law. Jesus also knew the very intentions of their hearts, to make this woman a public example so that the seventh commandment **"Thou shall not commit adultery" be honored, but they neglected the sixth commandment that says "Thou shall not murder".** Jesus knew that killing this woman was not the answer to her sin and therefore Jesus decided to raise the bar above the Law and grant forgiveness, mercy and love. Thank you Father for your love.

We see that Jesus took a position of humility when He stooped down and wrote on the ground with His finger. He behaved as if he didn't hear them, but He did. He heard them. He heard the woman's heart. He heard the Law written on stones. He heard the accusations of the Pharisees. He heard the heartbeat of his Heavenly Father and still chose to herald love to this woman. In verse 7 the accusers continued their taunting and finally Jesus stood up and responded:

"He who is without sin among you, let him throw a stone at her first." And again He stooped down and wrote on the ground. Then those who heard it, <u>being convicted by their conscience,</u> went out one by one, beginning with the oldest event to the last.

We don't know what Jesus wrote on the ground, but we can see that **<u>He rewrote the destiny of this woman from death to life.</u>** Jesus knew His purpose, to save the people in the world from their sins, and in this woman's case, she had a divine appointment with the the Resurrection and the Life although faced with the condemnation of death by stoning. Jesus saved this woman through love, mercy and forgiveness, trumped the consequence of death by stoning, and took her out of her dark adulterous rooms of despair so that she could experience a new type of life. She was translated from an impending doom of death to new life in Christ Jesus. The scribes came with the Law, but Jesus the righteous Judge and the Law Giver, knew all the do's and don'ts of the Law and with one simple response the Law wasn't mentioned by any of this woman's accusers. They left one by one being convicted in their conscience. Why? Notice, Jesus didn't tell them that they were right and the woman was wrong. He simply turned the tables on them. Yes, she committed a sin that broke the Law, but Jesus knew that they were not sinless either. They too committed sins that broke the Law, however they weren't caught in their acts as she was. Yes Father, your grace is enough.

Jesus is remarkable, glorious, wonderful, awesome and magnificent. He knows how to get our attentions with scenarios, circumstances and simple words. His response to the woman's accusers was: ***"He who is without sin among you, let him throw a stone at her first"***. This response impacted them because he responded to the condition of their hearts. He responded to their secret sins. He responded to their lifestyle. I can imagine the hush, the silence, the pause in time that enveloped the temple. The King of kings and Lord of lords pierced every demon that occupied the space. They groveled for this woman's blood and soul. She would have inevitably ended up in hell, but she was extended mercy, granted forgiveness, enveloped with love and saved by her Savior Jesus Christ. Love spoke up for her and rescued her.

Forgiveness wiped away her past. Her future was re written because Jesus didn't come to earth to condemn her but to save her. Hallelujah to the Lamb of God!

The event unfolds even more. When all the convicted accusers left, the woman was left alone with Jesus. She was standing. Jesus rose up from his stooping position and said:

"Woman, where are those accuser of yours? Has no one condemned you?" She said, "No one, Lord" And Jesus said to her, "Neither do I condemn you; go and sin no more."

Here we see the real personal encounter with Jesus. *He questions her: "Where are they that have accused and attempted to condemn you?" and she responds: "No one has condemned me Lord".* Imagine how her heart was beating rapidly because of a previous impending death sentence and now she was looking into the loving holy eyes of her loving powerful Savior, the One who defended her, reversed the judgment, brought her peace and set her free. Our God is Awesome. He can move mountains.

Yet, Jesus said something that culminated the event: <u>**"Neither do I condemn you so go and sin no more"**</u> This is the pontification of the event. Jesus proved His matchless love to this woman, knowing that according to Law, her sin was deserving death by stoning. He chose to show her that no matter what she had done, how many times she had done it, with whom and where, the love of God is limitless, abounding with mercy, steep with forgiveness and has no condemnation. Glory to God in the Highest for His love, mercy and forgiveness. Allow me to share a personal reflection.

Personal Reflection:

There were many times in my life I engaged in behaviors that were not pleasing in the Lord's sight. I knew better, knowing the Scriptures like we all do, but sometimes we desire to go ahead and do what we wish. The awesome thing that God had to show me was this: All things work together for good and the things that we battle with privately, when we finally master them and overcome, we can use our experiences to help others. There are hundreds of thousands and possibly millions of believers who struggle with "something". Whether it be adultery, pornography, fornication, drinking too much alcohol, drugging, gluttony, overspending, cussing up a storm, un-forgiveness, backbiting, hatred, impatience, or some other issue, if you check your baggage well, you will find out that you are not so squeaky clean. We all live in a world where people tend to pretend and act "perfect" but we all have challenges and imperfections, whether we hide them or be transparent about them. God doesn't want us to struggle in secrecy or be stoned in public. Jesus loves us and simply wants us to come to Him face to face in prayer and tell Him all that we struggle with. He will help us and we simply need to endure the process. The process may take 2days, 2 weeks, 2 years, 2 years or even 20 years God will help us with our thorns. Your struggle and process may not be identical to mine, but we do have some struggle. We simply need to ask God for His help and surrender to the process. If you think you don't have a struggle, you may not see it today, but it will show up somewhere within the next few weeks, months or years from now. God has a way of seeing us through our private challenges and our temple accusations. Know for sure that there will be an appointment with Jesus that when we encounter Him, he will defend us, stoop down and rescue us, tell our accusers to cast the first stone if he/she is without sin and then whisper in our ears: **"Neither do I condemn you. Go and sin no more."**

Let us Pray:

Heavenly Father, many are the struggles that I face. There are things in my life that are hidden from others but open to you. You know the whole truth about me. Lord, I thank you that you don't condemn or judge me as accusers would, for you didn't come to condemn but to extend mercy love and forgiveness. Lord help me to overcome the sins of _____ and help me now Lord and Master to surrender to the process so that I can live free from sin. Just as you didn't condemn the woman caught in adultery, thank you Lord for not condemning me. Help me to recognize when you are helping me to manage my weaknesses for you are my strength when I am weak. Help me Lord to daily go and sin no more. This I ask of you Lord in Jesus name Amen.

Freedom from Guilt
for we are Forgiven

Face to Face with Jesus

We recognized how the woman who was caught in the act of adultery gained a new life because she came face to face with Jesus Christ. Although her dark actions were exposed, the King of king didn't condemn her, but saved her from death and gave her new life in Him. She was forgiven and so are we. When we come face to face with our Creator, Master, King and Savior we are granted forgiveness. It is up to us to accept the gift of forgiveness and not carry the burden of guilt. We can live free from guilt for we are forgiven.

God's amazing love, mercy and forgiveness towards people through Jesus is displayed continuously in the Scriptures. God is also in the business of transformation. As

Believers, we are witnesses how Jesus moved and transformed our lives. Somehow, even when our lives are radically transformed, some people have a difficult time releasing guilt. Many get caught in a negative mindset, seized and pilfered by the spirit of not forgiving themselves. This is a reality for many. There are many people in this world who have committed or are still committing sins that plague their psyche. They simply cannot let it go. I was one of those people until God had to show me to **"Let go and let God."**

You may ask: "Let go and let God? What does that mean?" Some will mumble under their breath and say: "Easy for you to say Sister Heather" and I say to you: "You are right" Letting go and letting God take control is easier said than done. It is a deep process especially when it comes to forgiving yourself.

I will never forget a comment a professor made that riveted my life for the good. I mentioned it before. She said: **"Guilt is the biggest waste of time."** Some may hooray at this statement and others may boo at it, but it certainly made me jump a very huge hurdle in my life. This statement I paired with a Scripture in First John.

Read 1 John 1 vs 8 to 10. It states:

"If we say that we have no sin, we deceive ourselves, and the truth is not in us. If we confess our sins, He is faithful and just to forgive us our sins and

to cleanse us from all unrighteousness. If we say that we have not sinned, we make Him a liar, and His word is not in us."

Now this Scripture is a wakeup call for many. It certainly was for me. You see, all men on earth have sinned and fallen short of the glory of God. We will all do something that is not pleasing in the eyes of the Lord, whether we are aware of it or not. The problem lies when we intentionally sin and continue to sin as if it is the right thing to do. God doesn't want us to be burdened with guilty consciences for He knows that sin carries consequences and we tend to know (even young children) when we are doing or about to do the wrong thing. God has made a way to help us to release the burden of sin. We are to confess our sins and ask God to cleanse us from all unrighteousness. We should also ask God to strengthen us to keep us away from committing sin so that we can grow more in godliness and righteousness.

It was never God's intent for us to walk around feeling guilty of sins done whether it be the last hour, last night, last month, last year or last whenever. Guilt is what some people hold on to in order to remind themselves that they deserve the "beatings of life" In essence, guilt is not forgiving yourself and my questions to you is this: Why should you not forgive yourself? Isn't what's past in the past? Is holding yourself hostage to the past really going to change what happened? If God says you are forgiven, then consider God's word as final authority over your life. Never believe contrary to what God has said. **<u>If God forgives you, who are you not to forgive yourself?</u>**

It's one thing to admit sins, but another thing to forgive yourself of them. There are many who constantly sin without feeling any sort of remorse. Some of these people have deep psychological issues and are considered numb when it comes to feelings. But for those who sin and do not want to admit sin, they are in a grave place.

"If we say we have no sin we deceive ourselves and the truth is not in us."

We don't fool anyone when we say we have no sin. We only deceive ourselves and are outright liars. Liars have no place in the kingdom of God. God cannot use liars, for liars only speak their father's language. Satan is the father of lies. When lies are in operation, then that person is choosing to speak the language of satan. It is always best to see our situations from God's point of view which is displayed in the Scriptures. If God says a certain action is sinful, don't mask it and claim it is not, for in doing so, we simply deceive ourselves and the truth is not in us.

Admitting sins is humbly going to God and asking him for forgiveness. God knows us well and really loves to help us. He also knows that we shouldn't eat the devil's food of deception of not forgiving ourselves. When we chose not to forgive ourselves we can end up depressed and worse yet sick. Guilt is like a cancer, an awful reminder that gnaws at your inner being, constantly reminding you of the wrong, rather that reminding you of the forgiveness, mercy and love God has granted. The Scripture states:

"If we confess our sins, He is faithful and just to forgive us our sins and cleanse us from all unrighteousness."

God is the only one allowed to forgive us from our sins. Yes He is. He is the only One who can cleanse us from all unrighteousness. This shows that sin places us in a position of jeopardy therefore, we need to be repositioned by God. It is up to us to confess, open up our heart and mouth and humbly go to God and tell Him that we have done wrong. He is faithful to His Word and faithful to us to grant forgiveness. Now if God said this in His word and God is not a liar, (for it is impossible for Him to lie), then why is it we have trouble believing that God will forgive us? And if we believe that God has forgiven us, why is it we superimpose our guilt over God's mercy, love and forgiveness? Again I ask of you: Who are we not to forgive ourselves if God has forgiven us? Are we therefore bigger than God to not forgive ourselves? Know this for sure: God knew when we were going to sin. God knows our weaknesses. God understands our struggles. God sees that we are still growing. God is loving enough to teach us a better way but we must be willing to surrender and reach out to Him for help. God loves us too much to leave us in guilt and condemnation to wither away slowly in it. It's time to forgive yourself. Ask God to help you to do so.

Let us pray:

"Heavenly Father, we need thee every hour of every day. We need to understand the beauty of living a life in Christ Jesus, free from intentional sins, guilt and condemnation. Help us Lord to forgive ourselves and to enjoy the grace of your forgiveness, mercy and love. When we sin against you, teach us to repent immediately and humbly turn away from sin. As we move closer to you Lord allow us to cast away all shame and guilt, so that we can wear the garments of praise and thanksgiving knowing that your grace and your love for us is enough. This we pray in Jesus name Amen."

A Cry from the Heart for Mercy-Deliverance from Bondage

Earlier, we learned how the unmerciful servant was unmoved by the forgiveness granted to him by the king, who forgave him from an exorbitant about of debt. You see, when our hearts are not truly impacted by mercy and forgiveness extended to us by others, then we do not have the unction nor the ability to show likewise mercy and forgiveness to others. This was clear with the case of the unmerciful servant.

I believe it takes understanding one's position of need in order to accept and be grateful for mercy. When a person is in dire need, when mercy and love shows up, it impacts and also transforms that person in several ways. That person may be liberated from spiritual death to freedom, from darkness to light and from hatred to love. **When a person realizes that they need to move from being fractured to wholeness, from crutches to independence and from pain to purpose, they will cry out for MERCY**. Mercy in this case in layman's term means: **HELP ME PLEASE!!!!** This was what a blind beggar named Bartimaeus did in Mark 10 vs 46-52.

Read Mark 10 vs. 46-52

What impacted you the most in this biblical event? How do you feel about Bartimaeus? Do you think he was desperate? What are your thoughts about Jesus? Journalize.

_____

When Bartimaeus heard that Jesus was present, what did he do?

_____

Although Bartimaeus was told to be quiet, what did he do?

_____

Jesus was touched by this beggar's cry. What did Jesus do and say?

_____

What did Jesus ask Bartimaeus?

_____

How did Bartimaeus respond?

_____

Was Bartimaeus' request granted?

_____

Complete verse 52

And _____ he received his _____ and

_____ Jesus in the _____.

This biblical event explains how a desperate blind beggar who cried out to Jesus for mercy had a major miraculous encounter that changed his life for the better. Bartimaeus had a need and he wanted it bad. This man understood his position, and he needed a change….pronto. He understood that not only was he blind but also a beggar. This means Bartimaeus had to depend on the generosity and alms of others in order to survive. Who knows? Maybe Bartimaeus got tired of his situation of bondage to blindness and poverty and was desperate for a change. His change, his chance, his opportunity came when Jesus was about to leave Jericho. Bartimaeus decided in his head that there was no way Jesus was going to leave without using what he had power to do to gain what Jesus had the power to do for him. This blind beggar was dependent on a power that made him survive thus far….the power to beg with his mouth, using his tongue to cry out for help. Begging was his way to get what he needed and therefore he was going to beg Jesus to have **MERCY** on him.

"Jesus, Son of David, have mercy on me!" was Bartimaeus' cry.

He didn't cry out for his eyes to be healed. He cried out for **"MERCY"**. The word **MERCY** means to have compassion or forgiveness towards someone. In essence, if someone is crying out to another for mercy, then the crier is aware that the hearer is in some sort of position or has power to help. In Bartimaeus' case, I am sure he had heard about Jesus and the miracles he had performed and so even when he was being hushed by others to be quiet, Bartimaeus cried out even MORE for MERCY. Bartimaeus had faith that Jesus could and would help him.

Now, when Bartimaeus cried out, we don't know exactly what he wanted. It could have been money or food, but we see what Bartimaeus really needed when he came face to face with the Light of the World, Jesus Christ. Although Bartimaeus, the blind beggar, didn't see the face of Jesus initially when brought to Jesus, he walked away from his blindness with new vision. Hallelujah. When we come face to face with Jesus, our life changes. Let's see what occurred when Jesus spoke with Bartimaeus.

Jesus asked this beggar one question and this was the turning point for him.

"What do you want me to do for you?" Jesus asked him.

"To regain my sight." Bartimaeus responded

Isn't it amazing how Bartimaeus cried out for mercy but when asked what he wanted, he requested to see again? Now I couldn't help but to wonder, what does mercy have to do with sight? I couldn't help but to wonder how this beggar lost his sight. Did he lose his sight at birth? Was it because of sin he lost his sight? Did he injure his eyes by doing the wrong thing? Did he lost vision for his life? What made Bartimaeus blind? We may not have the exact answer to the reasons why Bartimaeus became blind, but we are comforted to know that he knew what to do to change his position.....to cry out to Jesus for MERCY. He knew that regaining his sight would radically change his life from darkness to light, from being a beggar to a follower of Jesus, from being in bondage to freedom, from being dependent on alms to independence and from being poor to being sustained. Jesus proves he has the power to do for us and for anyone who trusts in Him and who asks for mercy.

I am reminded of Isaiah 42 vs 6c to 7ab which describes Jesus, as *"a light to the Gentiles, to open blind eyes, to bring out prisoners from the prison,…"* This is what Jesus did for Bartimaeus. He showed compassion to him and opened his eyes, not only from physical blindness, but also from spiritual darkness. Bartimaeus regained what he had lost. He regained his sight to see the world, to see Jesus and to experience a new life in Christ. Jesus always gives us words of hope and encouragement and His words transform our lives. Jesus spoke these words to this once blind beggar:

"Go your way. Your faith has made you well"

Although Jesus told Bartimaeus to *"go your way"*, we notice in verse 52 that Bartimaeus followed Jesus *in the way*. Why? Answer: How could Bartimaeus continue on *in his way*, a prior life of begging and poverty, when he was now aware of a new way of life with his sight being restored? He had a change of heart and mind and decided **"I have to follow Jesus".** When we come to Christ, we cannot walk in the same darkness. We decide: **I have to follow Jesus in the way.**

This biblical event is one where we can apply to our very own lives. We may not be physically blind as Bartimaeus was, but spiritually blind, in the darkness of our own way and in bondage by the different systems of this world. Whether it being in a prison of success, depression, un-forgiveness, hate, lack, torment, emptiness, hurt, pain, poisoned thinking, the past, abuse, abortion, sickness, witchcrafts, evil morals, alcohol, sex, debt, fractured relationships or what have you, God desires that we be free from it. Whatever the situation, no matter how hurt you are, you can regain peace, freedom, set free from what seeks to chip away at you. There is no prison door or dungeon that is too hard or deep that God can't rescue you from. **In Jeremiah 32 vs.26- 27 GOD said HIMSELF to Jeremiah: Then the word of the Lord came to Jeremiah saying, "Behold, I AM THE LORD, the GOD of all flesh, Is there anything TOO HARD FOR ME?"** This Scripture can be our daily bread to carry us through the rest of our lives! We need to cry out to Jesus, Son of David, to have mercy on us, to help us and deliver us, for there is **NOTHING TOO HARD FOR GOD.** As seen in the Scriptures, Bartimaeus regained his sight and you can regain a new vision and a new life in Christ Jesus. **Receive your sight and new life in Jesus name!**

Let us Pray:

"Heavenly Father, you are the God of mercy, forgiveness and love. I have come to the realization that I am in a spiritual position that has blinded me and that desires to keep me in spiritual poverty and bondage. I need to regain

my spiritual vision Lord and I cannot regain it without your help. As blind Bartimaeus cried: Jesus, Son of David, have mercy on me! I am asking you Lord to have MERCY ON ME. Come face to face with me Lord and deliver me. Father, grant me new vision and a new life by releasing me from all that seeks to bind and blind me so that I can follow you in the way. This I pray in Jesus name Amen."

Loved By God-The Right Angle Effect-The Ultimate Sacrifice

Love encapsulates the concept and the movement of mercy and forgiveness. It takes divine love to extend mercy and forgiveness to others. In order to move forward in our spiritual life one has to grow in love.

It is not a mystery when God said that we are to love God with all our hearts, have no other God before him and to love others as we love ourselves. In loving God, not out of duty but out of purity, we will choose to put Him first. In observing how our relationship with our Heavenly Father develops and we witness His love towards us, we come to realize our value and the value of others. God doesn't abuse or devalue those whom He loves. God didn't create us to hate us. His intentions is always loving towards us. When we truly understand our intrinsic and extrinsic value, the value we hold in God's eyes, we will honor and love God, honor and love ourselves and others. True love is always shown in actions. We will review this later on in First Corinthians 13

The Right Angle Effect

The **"Love God, Love Yourself and Love Others Concept"** is what I term the ***"Right Angle Effect." This concept takes the shape of the letter "L".*** And for those of you who remember the right angled triangle, the angle's measurement is 90 degrees. Look at the words of the concept in bold. We see the "L" word there three times. *Love*. We are to love **God, Ourselves** and **Others**. But it first starts with God. ***Everything must begin with God for He is our very beginning.*** To write an "L" we start with the vertical line "I". At the head of this line we place God. At the end of the vertical line we place ourselves. Our relationship between us and God must be straight before we can extend love to others, which is the horizontal part which completes the "L". We ought to love God and allow God to pour His love on us. When we do this, we maintain an open loving relationship between us and God. In return, God will design the correct relationships that we need to have in our lives. It is possible to develop open loving relationships with others free from perversions and ulterior motives. Love is not perverted. Love is pure, kind, not self-seeking, disturbed or abusive. God doesn't abuse or do wickedness to us, so never allow a deceptive lustful experience to creep into your life undercover posing as love. **The "Right Angle Effect" is a love relationship that is first vertical**

(God and you) then horizontal (you and others) which forms in an "L". At the intersection of the 90 degrees angle, this is our love temperature, where relationships between God, us and others are not too hot to kill us and not too cold to freeze us. Notice also that the point of reference where the vertical line meets the horizontal line is where we are positioned. We are the link of showing God's love to others. Amen.

God Loves You

God loves you. Yes you. God loves me. Yes me. Believe that. Receive that. The God of this universe thought of you and took the time to design and create the totality of who you are from the inside out. You are not a mistake and your life is not a tragedy. You are alive, reading this right now because God chose you to be here, today and He desires to do a new thing in your life. He wants to transform you just like He did at the marriage of Cana when He changed the water into wine.

Think about the miracles Jesus performed throughout the Gospels. Think about all the miraculous events which occurred through God's mighty Hand displayed in the Scriptures. God has been changing the lives of people throughout the ages to this present day. He is doing it even now in your life as you read this. You may not see the effects now, but it will show up later on. No matter what you are facing now, have faced in the past or will face in the future, God can and will re-write your story….if you let Him. He did it for the woman caught in the act of adultery, for Bartimaeus, for the nation of Israel who suffered under Egyptian bondage, for Moses, for Joshua, for Elijah, Rahab a harlot, Ruth, Esther, Boaz, Heather Hope Johnson and countless more. **HE CAN DO IT FOR YOU**.

God has awesome amazing powers. Too many to put in this book. The three we focused on were **MERCY, FORGIVENESS AND LOVE**.

GOD IS LOVE

God is LOVE. Look what First John 4: 16 states about God:

"And we have known and believed the love that God has for us. God is love, and he who abides in love abides in God, and God in him."

I have learned that whatever God does, the undergirding and foundation of His actions is LOVE, because LOVE defines God.

Ask yourself these questions and seek to answer them. Why did Jesus heal the sick, raise the dead, taught in parables, fed thousands and led the lost?

Answer:_____

Jesus saw the needs of the people and had compassion on them. In being moved by their burdens and dilemmas, He worked in the spirit of love, forgiveness and mercy to **HELP THEM. Love always seeks to HELP and led to help**.

Can you imagine being sick, hungry, lacking knowledge, perishing, confused, bound and have no direction for life? Yes. We have been there in various degrees at least once. Being in these positions of lack, sickness, confusion, trouble and need, spells **<u>DESPERATION</u>**. God saw the desperation of the people in the world and knew that we were like sheep without a shepherd. God saw the problem and sent the solution, Jesus the Good Shepherd who loves us to the very end, even on the cross.

<u>Love Sacrifice</u>

John 3:16 -17 is a very popular Scripture and I believe it is the heart beat, circulatory system and lifeblood of the entire Bible. It states:

> **"For God so loved the world that He gave His only begotten Son that whosoever believeth in Him shall not perish but shall have everlasting life. For God did not send his Son into the world to condemn the world, but in order that the world might be saved through him."**

This Scripture is self-explanatory and should not be over thought. God is not trying to play games with us or trying to trick us with a tale. This Scripture is the truth.

The entire Bible is the truth. God saw the condition of mankind in the world and decided to send a solution. The solution was and is still Jesus. Wars do not solve problems. Governments do not solve problems. Neither psychologists nor politicians cannot solve spiritual problems. Jesus always solved problems for His method is unlike the methods of the systems of this world. Jesus' system of solving problem is to **LOVE, for LOVE CONQUERS ALL**.

We witnessed how the adulteress caught in the act of adultery had a problem and although she was condemn to death by men because of a written "law", Jesus the problem solver, saved her and made her life new. Bartimaeus also had a problem. He was a blind beggar and although men wanted to hush him up, Jesus had mercy on him and saved him from his dilemma. Time and again many people in positions of need were delivered and saved because of Jesus the Savior. They had to put their faith in Jesus in order to have access to a new life. Will the people of this world who need a change of life choose to have a change of heart and ask Jesus to enter in and do a new work in their life? It is never too late for a new life. This world cannot give life eternal. Only God gives it. God doesn't work according to the world's standards. God is of a higher standard. The world's system will not deliver the same results as God's system. The world system seeks to solve issues in a way that promises only limited results. Man will never have unlimited powers like our Almighty God.

Works of the World System

You see, the problems of this world are many. Mankind with evil intentions create laws that are unjust which causes problems such as wars. When a solution is needed, these solutions are normally lopsided and unequal. If we notice the reasons behind problems in this world, they are normally centered in some sort of greed at the expense of innocent people. There is too much exploitation, oppression, condemnation and death occurring and it is all because of selfishness. Mankind create laws that often do not work, because mankind create solutions to suit themselves. The new command that Jesus gave was, **THE LAW of LOVE**. This command has been time tested and has always won and worked. Imagine a world where people come into agreement with the LAW of LOVE to do what needs to be done out of the Spirit of Love, Mercy and Forgiveness? Just as how many lives have been saved because of Jesus, your life can be saved also because Jesus loves you and wants to save you from an impending doom. It is never too late. Even if you are on your death bed reading this, you are still able to put your faith in Jesus and enter into eternal life. This is what happened to a thief on a cross in Luke 23 vs 33 to 43 who put his faith in Jesus.

Read Luke 23 vs 33-43 NASB or ESV

According to this Scripture answer the following questions.

Where was the place of crucifixion called? _____

What does a skull represent? _____

Who was being crucified alongside Jesus? _____

Are criminals guilty or innocent? _____

What did Jesus say in verse 34? _____

_____

Look at verses 35 to 39. The rulers scoffed Jesus. Soldiers mocked Jesus and one of the criminals railed out at Jesus. They all had a similar statement. Log them here.

The rulers:

_____

The soldiers: _____

The criminal: _____

The one common word (theme) amongst these people who lashed out at Jesus was the word (theme): _____.

Here we see a close view of what Jesus the King of the Jews endured while being on the cross. Nailed, bloody, bruised, hanging in pain, he was being jeered by different sets of people. Can you imagine how Jesus was being tortured emotionally in addition to being tortured physically? It was the maximum example of cruel and unusual punishment for no sin committed on His part. The message here that we must take with us about this event is what they said to Jesus and how they said it. *The rulers, soldiers and criminal all verbalized that Jesus should have used the power he had, to save himself from the anguish he was facing.* They mocked him stating that he had the power to **save** others, therefore he should use this same power to rescue himself. Not only did they say this, but they also used a tactic that satan used at the beginning of Christ's ministry.

Read Matthew 4 vs 4 to 10.

Satan had tempted Jesus three times in the wilderness by stating the following in **Matthew 4 vs 3, 6 and 9**:

Vs. 3: And the tempter came and said to him, **"If you are the Son of God**, command these stones to become loaves of bread"

Vs. 6: **"If you are the Son of God**, throw yourself down…"

Vs. 9: "All these I will give you, **if you will fall down and worship me."**

This tactic of questioning the identity of Jesus **was used by Satan at the beginning of Jesus' ministry. It was also present at the culmination of His ministry on the cross.** Satan showed up through the rulers, soldiers and that criminal stating in Luke 23 vs 35, 37 and 39:

Vs. 35 "…..but the rulers scoffed at him, saying, "He saved others; let him save himself, **if he is the Christ of God, his Chosen One!"**

Vs. 37: The soldiers also mocked him, coming up and offering him sour wine and saying, **"If you are the King of the Jews, save yourself!"**

Vs. 39: One of the criminals who were hanged railed at him, saying, **"Are you not the Christ? Save yourself and us!"**

Isn't it interesting how satan will show up with a vengeance to try to get us away from the purposes of God? You see, Jesus came from heaven to do the purpose of God and satan's intentions from the very beginning was to side track and overthrow the plans and purposes of God. Satan will use anyone, anything and whatever it takes to keep us in a pit all in an effort to plunder the purposes of God for our lives.

This is what the devil wanted to do. Distract Jesus from his purposes. But Jesus stood the course for He knew that the purpose of God was much greater and much more important than satisfying his needs and saving himself. **<u>The purpose of Jesus on earth was to save those who were lost and bring them into eternal life.</u>** His identity was being tested, because Satan wanted Jesus to prove to others that He was the Christ, the King of the Jews and the Chosen One of God. This was a test of the "pride of life" to prove his power and might, but Jesus didn't fall for it. Jesus already knew who He was and others already witnessed His power and believed, so even if the criminal, the rulers and the soldiers didn't believe, it was too late. That part of his journey was over. Jesus was too close to victory to fall into a "pride of life trap" and so He had to stay the course of His Father's will. Jesus knew that it wasn't about him. It was about the people of the world that needed the chance to gain eternal life through his sacrificial and redemptive work. Amen.

There is one more thing I learned with this biblical event and it's this: Even when Satan rails, mocks, shouts and carries on, God has a way of speaking up and defending us if we remain humble and in the spirit of love. God showed up in this case through the other criminal on the cross in **Luke 23 vs 40-43**.

Read Luke 23 vs. 40 -43

We see where the other criminal on the cross was in the right state of mind and state of heart. This criminal rebuked the other criminal who railed out at Jesus.

What did this criminal say in Luke 23 vs 40 -41?

You see, this criminal understood his position. He knew that he was being punished for his criminal activity. He knew that Jesus was not a criminal as he was. I am certain he heard the reason behind Jesus' sentence and knew it was not deserving of the death penalty. He must have observed the evil at work against Jesus who was innocent, yet no record of rebuke and mockery was being thrown at him being a criminal. He must have been impacted at the humility of Jesus on the cross, bearing his punishment without backlashing at his torturers and tormentors. This criminal was so moved at what he witnessed he turned to Jesus and said in verse 42:

"Jesus, remember me when you come into your kingdom."

This criminal took a bold step. He had faith to believe that Jesus indeed was the King of the Jews, the Chosen One, and the Christ of God that he wanted to be with Jesus in His kingdom. He witnessed the difference in Jesus, his demeanor, his attitude, his presence during the entire crucifixion. This criminal witnessed love in action on the cross. Jesus didn't ask this criminal to come to his kingdom, but what the criminal experienced *made him want to be with Jesus in His kingdom*. Jesus responded to this criminal by stating:

"Truly, I say to you, today you will be with me in Paradise,"

All I can say right here is WOW! Here we see this criminal on the cross, condemn to death by a law. He would have probably ended up in hell for his crime committed, but **LOVE** stepped in. Jesus didn't evangelize to this criminal on the cross, but Jesus' attitude spoke volumes to this criminal to the extent that he spoke up for Jesus, correcting the other criminal and then turned to Jesus and asked him to remember him. In essence, this criminal was asking for mercy and forgiveness in an unusual way. *This criminal didn't say the sinner's prayer but Jesus saw the sincerity in his heart, looked beyond his crime and granted him definite access to be with Him in Paradise that very day*. I am amazed at this because it only shows that even at death's door, as a criminal, we can ask God for forgiveness and mercy and our loving Savior will see the sincerity in our hearts and will grant us access to Heaven to be with Him eternally. Glory to the King of kings and Lord of lords.

The Power of Love

The crucifixion of Jesus Christ was the ultimate sacrifice and power of love God did for mankind. It was a sacrificial act on Jesus' part, but a cruel and inhumane method designed by man for no sin committed by Jesus. You see, the rulers and those involved thought that killing the Son of God was going to kill the message of the Gospel of the Kingdom. Instead, the message was magnified.

The life purpose of Jesus was to come into the world filled with people who were broken in order to restore them. Their lives were broken from fellowship and communion with God. In addition, due to the God-man fractured fellowship, all decisions made by man were not aligned with God's will. Mankind had no proper guidance and was living like sheep without a shepherd. Jesus was the answer God sent to be the bridge that mankind needed to access oneness with God to live a full life instead of a fractured one. Those who accept the gift of salvation through Jesus will have life eternal. Those who do not accept God's gift of salvation will have a condemned life despite whether they believe in Jesus or not.

Mankind's Basic Need

Love is what every human being needs and desires. Notice how people respond to love and kindness. Love is definitely a component that we have been designed to need. When we are loved, we thrive. When we are loved, we blossom. When we are loved we feel, look and behave differently. There is something about LOVE that makes us LEAP from the inside out. **Our food for thought here is this: God loves His children very much. God desires the very best for His children. God knows that there is no one on this planet who can love us more than He can.** As humans, we tend to trust and love others more than we love God and this is where we get into problems. It is our wrong choices that propels us into static and sticky situations as it relates to loving. God said that we are to love HIM with ALL our heart, soul, mind and strength. We cannot love others more than we love God because when people disappoint us it can wreck us. God will not treat us as how people do. People at times get fickle with their feelings or bored with us and will quickly move on with their lives in a heartbeat. These actions often leave people with broken hearts and disturbed minds. **<u>Know this for sure: When others stop loving us, God will not stop loving us</u>**. Despite the messes and bad choices we have made, God will wipe away our tears, heal our hearts and help us to move forward again.

<u>Take this advice: Love God with your all and allow God to lead the right people to love you in return.</u>

<u>The Proof is in the Word</u>

As we approach the end of this intimate bible study, I hope you have learned much about the mercy, forgiveness and love of God. We have seen how God has proven His power over and over in the Scriptures and it is really up to us to receive and believe. Where we spend eternity is entirely up to us. Do you know that no one has power over your choices? If you choose to hand over your power to choose to satanic influences, the outcome will be a disastrous one. Choose whom you will serve today. Will you choose Jesus the Son of God or satan the destroyer of mankind?

The bible is NOT a fairytale. It is a collection of realities of real events, real people who experienced real deliverances. We may not have been present many centuries ago, but we can feel, sense and connect with these people and their experiences. Even when we look at the trajectory of our lives, we see what God has done for us because God loves us. It's that simple. What has God done for you? Can you answer that?

What has he rescued you from? What has God provided for you? What has God protected you from? How has God delivered you? How did God send His divine messages to you? Yes, think about it. God is real. God is real. God is real. God did all what He did JUST FOR YOU because HE LOVES YOU!

A Final Note-Love Never Fails

We have journeyed together and viewed the mercy, forgiveness and love of God through the Scriptures. There is one more Scripture that I want to leave with you and it hails from **First Corinthians 13 vs. 4 to 8a**. This Scriptures gives us details of what love is and what it is not. When we see these characteristics of love, then we will know for sure that we are in the presence of the spirit of love, the spirit of GOD.

Read First Corinthian 13 vs. 4 to 8a.

Write all the things that describes love. (include also what love isn't)

Love is (isn't): _____

_____

_____

_____

First Corinthians 13 vs. 8a: Love _____ fails.

When I read this Scripture all I see is the character and example of Jesus. The word that I can use to sum up love is **"purity"**. Love is pure and I am so settled in my heart that God who is Love, is also pure and free from anything evil. God's love is so amazingly powerful and I can only imagine how God's perspective on a situation is exceptionally different from ours. When we see the effects of sin grappling an individual, God sees the potential in that individual and how He can transform them only if they put their faith in Him. He did it with Bartimaeus, the adulterous woman and the criminal on the cross.

Nothing evil and unrighteous can abide or dwell in God's presence. God is so holy and powerful that if anything that is unlike Him should come into His presence, it has to bow or flee. We see this happening when the hurting or sick came in the presence of Jesus. When sickness, evil, lack or anyone who suffered came in the presence of Jesus, transformation took place. It couldn't remain the same especially if the person truly desired to change and expressed that even with minimal faith.

Love never fails.

Love never fails. It never fails. Why? God cannot fail. Love will always win over hate and evil. Love is power at its peak. Full voltage. The power of love is not destructive, but redemptive. When we truly decide to allow God to fill us with His love, nothing evil can overcome us because evil has to either bow to love, flee from love or submit to love. Evil is weakened by love because God conquers all. **Know this for sure: When we determine to walk in love we will always win the heart of mankind because LOVE CONQUERS ALL.**

We have come to the end of this Bible study but entering into a new beginning of walking in the mercy, forgiveness and love of God. Remember that this is a process alongside the Holy Spirit. It cannot be accomplished solely with human effort, however, if we choose to surrender our will so that God's will can operate through us, then we can do all things through Jesus Christ who strengthens us.

Let us Pray:

Heavenly Father, I thank you for allowing me to journey through this intimate Bible Study. I have gained revelations through your Word, by your Holy Spirit

and I ask that you will allow me to maintain what I have learned so that I can walk in the spirit of mercy, forgiveness and the love of God. Teach me again and again O Lord, how to live this life in Christ Jesus, so that honor is given to you through my life. Use me Lord as You have used others. Bless me and grant me all that I need to live a life of victory, humility, love and peace each day. This I pray Father in Jesus name Amen.

Isaiah 55 vs 11

"So shall My word be that goes forth from My mouth; It shall not return to Me void, But it shall accomplish what I please, and it shall prosper in the thing for which I sent it."